Y0-ABR-742

A TREASURY OF AUSTRALIAN VERSE

The
MAN
FROM
SNOWY
RIVER
& OTHER CLASSICS

The Five Mile Press

CONTENTS

INTRODUCTION

THE verse written by Australia's 19th-century and early 20th-century poets played an important role in shaping the young nation's sense of identity. 'Banjo' Paterson gave us a mythical hero in 'The Man from Snowy River' as well as our unofficial national anthem 'Waltzing Matilda'.

And a 19-year-old girl, Dorothea Mackellar, struck a national chord with her poem 'My Country' in 1904.

Charles Harpur, Henry Kendall, Adam Lindsay Gordon, Barcroft Boake, C.J. Dennis, and Henry Lawson are among the other poets who helped us to see ourselves and our country through their verse.

This nostalgic collection of poems — by both famous poets and unknown versifiers — evokes the hardships of Outback life, and the spirit of our early settlers.

THE MAN FROM SNOWY RIVER

THERE was movement at the station,
   for the word had passed around
That the colt from old Regret had
   got away,
And had joined the old bush horses
   — he was worth a thousand pound,
So all the cracks had gathered to the
   fray.
All the tried and noted riders from
   the stations near and far
Had mustered at the homestead
   overnight,

For the bushmen love hard riding
    where the old bush horses are,
And the stock-horse snuffs the battle
    with delight.

There was Harrison, who made his
    pile when Pardon won the cup,
The old man with his hair as white
    as snow;
But few could ride beside him when
    his blood was fairly up —
He would go wherever horse and
    man could go.
And Clancy of the Overflow came
    down to lend a hand,
No better horseman ever held the
    reins;

For never horse could throw him
   while the saddle-girths would stand —
He learnt to ride while droving on
   the plains.

And one was there, a stripling on a
   small and weedy beast;
He was something like a racehorse
   undersized,
With a touch of Timor pony — three
   parts thoroughbred at least —
And such as are by mountain horsemen prized.
He was hard and tough and wiry —
   just the sort that won't say die —
There was courage in his quick
   impatient tread;

And he bore the badge of gameness
   in his bright and fiery eye,
And the proud and lofty carriage of
   his head.

But still so slight and weedy, one
   would doubt his power to stay,
And the old man said, 'That horse
   will never do
For a long and tiring gallop — lad,
   you'd better stop away,
Those hills are far too rough for such
   as you.'
So he waited sad and wistful — only
   Clancy stood his friend —
'I think we ought to let him come.'
   he said;

'I warrant he'll be with us when he's
      wanted at the end,
For both his horse and he are
      mountain bred.

'He hails from Snowy River, up by
      Kosciusko's side,
Where the hills are twice as steep
      and twice as rough;
Where a horse's hoofs strike firelight
      from the flint stones every stride,
The man who holds his own is
      good enough.
And the Snowy River riders on the
      mountains make their home,
Where the river runs those giant hills
      between;

I have seen full many horsemen since
    I first commenced to roam,
But nowhere yet such horsemen have
    I seen.'

So he went; they found the horses by
    the big mimosa clump,
They raced away towards the
    mountain's brow,
And the old man gave his orders,
    'Boys, go at them from the jump,
No use to try for fancy riding now.
And, Clancy, you must wheel them,
    try and wheel them to the right.
Ride boldly, lad, and never fear the
    spills,

For never yet was rider that could
    keep the mob in sight,
If once they gain the shelter of those
    hills.'

So Clancy rode to wheel them — he
    was racing on the wing
Where the best and boldest riders
    take their place,
And he raced his stock-horse past
    them, and he made the ranges ring
With the stockwhip, as he met them
    face to face.
Then they halted for a moment, while
    he swung the dreaded lash,
But they saw their well-loved mount-
    ains full in view,

And they charged beneath the stockwhip with a sharp and sudden dash,
And off into the mountain scrub they
flew.

Then fast the horsemen followed,
where the gorges deep and black
Resounded to the thunder of their
tread,
And the stockwhips woke the echoes,
and they fiercely answered back
From cliffs and crags that beetled
overhead.
And upward, ever upward, the wild
horses held their way,
Where mountain ash and kurrajong
grew wide;

And the old man muttered fiercely,
  'We may bid the mob good day,
No man can hold them
    down the other side.'

When they reached the mountain's
    summits, even Clancy took a pull —
It well might make the boldest hold
    their breath;
The wild hop scrub grew thickly, and
    the hidden ground was full
Of wombat holes, and any slip was
    death.
But the man from Snowy River let
    the pony have his head,
And he swung his stockwhip round
    and gave a cheer,

And he raced him down the mountain
   like a torrent down its bed,
While the others stood and watched
   in very fear.

He sent the flint stones flying, but
   the pony kept his feet,
He cleared the fallen timber in his
   stride,
And the man from Snowy River never
   shifted in his seat —
It was grand to see that mountain
   horseman ride.
Through the stringy-barks and saplings,
   on the rough and broken ground,
Down the hillside at a racing pace
   he went;

And he never drew the bridle till he
    landed safe and sound
At the bottom of that terrible descent.

He was right among the horses as
    they climbed the farther hill,
And the watchers on the mountain,
    standing mute,
Saw him ply the stockwhip fiercely;
    he was right among them still,
As he raced across the clearing
    in pursuit.
Then they lost him for a moment,
    where two mountain gullies met
In the ranges — but a final glimpse
    reveals

On a dim and distant hillside the
    wild horses racing yet,
With the man from Snowy River at
    their heels.

And he ran them single-handed till
   their sides were white with foam;
He followed like a bloodhound on
   their track,
Till they halted, cowed and beaten;
   then he turned their heads for home,
And alone and unassisted brought
   them back.
But his hardy mountain pony he
   could scarcely raise a trot,
He was blood from hip to shoulder
   from the spur;
But his pluck was still undaunted,
   and his courage fiery hot,
For never yet was mountain horse a cur.

And down by Kosciusko, where the
   pine-clad ridges raise
Their torn and rugged battlements
   on high,
Where the air is clear as crystal, and
   the white stars fairly blaze
At midnight in the cold and frosty sky,
And where around the Overflow the
   reed-beds sweep and sway
To the breezes, and the rolling plains
   are wide,
The man from Snowy River is a
   household word today,
And the stockmen tell the story of his
   ride.

—A.B. ('Banjo') Paterson—

WHERE THE DEAD MEN LIE

OUT on the wastes of the Never Never —
That's where the dead men lie!
There where the heat-waves dance
    for ever —
That's where the dead men lie!
That's where the Earth's loved sons
    are keeping
Endless Tryst: not the west wind
    sweeping
Feverish pinions can wake their
    sleeping —
Out where the dead men lie!

Where brown Summer and Death
   have mated —
That's where the dead men lie!
Loving with fiery lust unsated —
That's where the dead men lie!
Out where the grinning skulls bleach
   whitely
Under the saltbush sparkling
   brightly;
Out where the wild dogs chorus
   nightly —
That's where the dead men lie!

Deep in the yellow, flowing river —
That's where the dead men lie!
Under the banks where the shadows
   quiver —

That's where the dead men lie!
Where the platypus twists and
    doubles,
Leaving a train of tiny bubbles;
Rid at last of their earthly troubles —
That's where the dead men lie!

East and backward pale faces
    turning —
That's how the dead men lie!
Gaunt arms stretched with a
    voiceless yearning —
That's how the dead men lie!
Oft in the fragrant hush of nooning
Hearing again their mother's
    crooning,

Wrapt for aye in a dreamful
   swooning —
That's how the dead men lie!

Only the hand of Night can free them —
That's when the dead men fly!
Only the frightened cattle see them —
See the dead men go by!
Cloven hoofs beating out one
   measure,
Bidding the stockmen know no
   leisure —
That's when the dead men take
   their pleasure!
That's when the dead men fly!

Ask, too, the never-sleeping drover:
He sees the dead pass by;
Hearing them call to their friends —
    the plover,
Hearing the dead men cry;
Seeing their faces stealing, stealing,
Hearing their laughter peeling, peeling,
Watching their grey forms wheeling,
    wheeling
Round where the cattle lie!

Strangled by thirst and fierce
    privation —
That's how the dead men die!
Out on Moneygrub's farthest station —
That's how the dead men die!

Hard-faced greybeards, youngsters
    callow;
Some mounds cared for, some left
    fallow;
Some deep down, yet others
    shallow;
Some having but the sky.

Moneygrub, as he sips his claret,
Looks with complacent eye
Down at his watch-chain, eighteen
    carat —
There, in his club, hard by:
Recks not that every link is stamped
    with
Names of men whose limbs are
    cramped with

Too long lying in grave-mould
    cramped with
Death where the dead men lie.

—Barcroft Boake—

NINE MILES FROM GUNDAGAI

I'VE done my share of shearing
  sheep,
Of droving and all that,
And bogged a bullock-team as well,
On a Murrumbidgee flat.
I've seen the bullock stretch and
  strain,
And blink his bleary eye,
And the dog sit on the tucker box,
Nine miles from Gundagai.

I've been jilted, jarred, and crossed
  in love,
And sand-bagged in the dark,

Till if a mountain fell on me
I'd treat it as a lark.
It's when you've got your bullocks
     bogged
That's the time you flog and cry,
And the dog sits on the tucker box,
Nine miles from Gundagai.

We've all got our little troubles,
In life's hard, thorny way,
Some strike them in a motor car
And others in a dray.
But when your dog and bullocks
     strike
It ain't no apple pie,
And the dog sat on the tucker box
Nine miles from Gundagai.

But that's all past and dead and
    gone,
And I've sold the team for meat,
And perhaps some day where I was
    bogged,
There'll be an asphalt street.
The dog, ah! well he got a bait,
And thought he'd like to die,
So I buried him in the tucker box,
Nine miles from Gundagai.

—Jack Moses—

A CONVICT'S LAMENT

I AM a native of Erin's island
But banished now from my native
   shore;
They tore me from my aged parents,

And from the maiden I adore.
In transient storms as I set sailing,
Like mariner bold my course did
    steer;
Sydney Harbour was my destination —
That cursed place at length drew
    near.

I then joined banquet in congratu-
    lation
On my safe arrival from the briny sea;
But, Alas, Alas! I was mistaken —
Twelve years transportation to
    Moreton Bay!
Early one morning, as I carelessly
    wandered,

By the Brisbane waters I chanced to
    stray;
I heard a prisoner sadly bewailing,
Whilst on the sunny river-banks he lay.

He said: 'I've been a prisoner at Port
    Macquarie,
At Norfolk Island, and Emu Plains;
At Castle Hill and cursed
    Toongabbee —
At all those places I've worked in
    chains:
But of all the places of condemn-
    ation,
In each penal station of New South
    Wales,

To Moreton Bay I found no equal,
For excessive tyranny each day
  prevails.

Early in the morning when day is
  dawning,
To trace from heaven the morning
  dew,
Up we are started at a moment's
  warning,
Our daily labour to renew.
Our overseers and superintendents —
These tyrants' orders we must obey,
Or else at the triangles our flesh is
  mangled —
Such are our wages at Moreton Bay!

For three long years I've been
    beastly treated;
Heavy irons each day I wore;
My back from flogging has been
    lacerated,
And oftimes painted with crimson
    gore.
Like the Egyptians and ancient
    Hebrews,
We were oppressed under Logan's
    yoke,
Till kind Providence came to our
    assistance,
And gave this tyrant his mortal
    stroke.

Yes, he has hurried from that place
   of bondage,
Where he thought he would gain
   renown;
But a native black, who lay in
   ambush,
Gave this monster his fatal wound.
My fellow-prisoners, be exhilarated —
That all such monsters such a death
   may find:
For it's when from bondage we are
   extricated,
Our former sufferings will fade from
   mind.'

—Anon—

CONDAMINE BELLS

BY A forge near a hut on the
   Condamine River
A blacksmith laboured at his ancient
   trade;

With his hammer swinging and his
    anvil ringing
He fashioned bells from a crosscut
    blade.

And while he toiled by the
    Condamine River
He sang a song for a job well done;
And the song and the clamour of his
    busy hammer
Merged and mingled in a tempered
    tone.

And his bell rang clear from the
    Condamine River
To the Gulf, to the Leeuwin, over soil
    and sand;

Desert eagles winging heard his
stock-bells ringing
As a first voice singing in a songless
land.

The smith is lost to the Condamine
River,
Gone is the humpy where he used
to dwell;
But the songs and the clamour of his
busy hammer
Ring on through the land in the
Condamine Bell.

—Jack Sorensen—

MY COUNTRY

THE love of field and coppice,
Of green and shaded lanes,
Of ordered woods and gardens
Is running in your veins.
Strong love of grey-blue distance,
Brown streams and soft, dim skies —
I know, but cannot share it,
My love is otherwise.

I love a sunburnt country,
A land of sweeping plains,
Of ragged mountain ranges,
Of droughts and flooding rains.
I love her far horizons,
I love her jewel-sea,

Her beauty and her terror —
The wide brown land for me!

The stark white ring-barked forests,
All tragic to the moon,
The sapphire-misted mountains,
The hot gold hush of noon,
Green tangle of the brushes
Where lithe lianas coil,
And orchids deck the tree tops,
And ferns the warm dark soil.

Core of my heart, my country!
Her pitiless blue sky,
When, sick at heart, around us
We see the cattle die —
But then the grey clouds gather,

And we can bless again
The drumming of an army,
The steady soaking rain.

Core of my heart, my country!
Land of the rainbow gold,
For flood and fire and famine
She pays us back threefold.
Over the thirsty paddocks,
Watch, after many days,
The filmy veil of greenness
That thickens as we graze...

An opal-hearted country,
A wilful, lavish land —
All you who have not loved her,
You will not understand —

Though Earth holds many splendours,
Wherever I may die,
I know to what brown country
My homing thoughts will fly.

—Dorothea Mackellar—

THE NEVER-NEVER LAND

BY hut, homestead, and
   shearing-shed,
By railroad, coach, and track —
By lonely graves where rest our dead,
Up-Country and Out-Back:

To where beneath the clustered stars
The dreamy plains expand —
My home lies wide a thousand miles
In the Never-Never Land.

It lies beyond the farming belt,
Wide wastes of scrub and plain,
A blazing desert in the drought,
A lake-land after rain;
To the skyline sweeps the waving
    grass,
Or whirls the scorching sand —
A phantom land, a mystic realm!
The Never-Never Land.

Where lone Mount Desolation lies,
Mounts Dreadful and Despair —

'Tis lost beneath the rainless skies
In hopeless deserts there;
It spreads nor'-west by No-Man's
    Land —
Where clouds are seldom seen —
To where the cattle-stations lie
Three hundred miles between.

The drovers of the Great Stock
    Routes
The strange Gulf country know —
Where, travelling from the southern
    droughts,
The big lean bullocks go;
And camped by night where plains
    lie wide,
Like some old ocean's bed,

The watchmen in the starlight ride
Round fifteen hundred head.

Lest in the city I forget
True mateship after all,
My water-bag and billy yet
Are hanging on the wall;
And I, to save my soul again,
Would tramp to sunsets grand
With sad-eyed mates across the plain
In the Never-Never Land.

—Henry Lawson—

CLICK GO THE SHEARS

OUT on the board the old shearer
  stands,
Grasping his shears in his long, bony
  hands;
Fixed is his gaze on a bare-bellied
  'joe',
Glory if he gets her, won't he make
  the 'ringer' go!

Chorus:
Click go the shears boys, click, click,
  click;
Wide is his blow and his hands
  move quick,

The ringer looks round and is
    beaten by a blow,
And curses the old snagger with his
    bare-bellied 'joe'.

In the middle of the floor, in his
    cane-bottomed chair
Is the boss of the board, with his
    eyes everywhere;
Notes well each fleece as it comes
    to the screen,
Paying strict attention if it's taken off
    clean.

The colonial experience man, he is
    there, of course,

With his shiny leggin's, just got off
  his horse;
Casting round his eye, like a real
  connoisseur,
Whistling the old tune, 'I'm the
  Perfect Lure.'

The tar-boy is there, awaiting in
  demand,
With his blackened tar-pot, and his
  tarry hand,
Sees one old sheep with a cut upon
  its back,
Hears what he's waiting for, 'Tar
  here, Jack!'

Shearing is all over and we've all got
  our cheques,
Roll up your swag boys, we're off on
  the tracks;
The first pub we come to, it's there
  we'll have a spree,
And everyone that comes along, it's
  'Have a drink with me!'

Down by the bar the old shearer
  stands,
Grasping his glass in his thin bony
  hands;
Fixed is his gaze on a green-painted
  keg,
Glory, he'll get down on it, ere he
  stirs a peg.

There we leave him standing,
  shouting for all hands,
Whilst all around him, every drinker
  stands:
His eyes are on the cask, which is
  now lowering fast,
He works hard, he drinks hard, and
  goes to hell at last!

—Anon—

COUNTRY FELLOWS

WHEN country fellows come to town,
And meet to have a chat,
They bring the news from Camperdown,
Birchip and Ballarat.
Wisely they talk of wheat and wool
From Boort and Buningyong,
From Warragul and Warrnambool,
From Junee and Geelong.

Ted tells them how the crops are now
Well up round Bullarook,
And Fred describes the champion
cow
He bred at Quambatook.
'If rain comes soon, 'twill be a boon,'

Says Clive of Koo-wee-rup.
'Too right,' says Nick of Nar-nar-goon;
'The grass wants fetchin' up.'

And I, who have been country bred,
And love the country still,
I listen wistfully to Ted
And George and Joe and Bill.
I see again the peaceful scene,
I hear them talk of paddocks green,
At Yea and Grogan's Dam,
Koroit, Kerang and Moulamein;
Then, dreaming of the
might-have-been,
I go home in a tram.

—C.J. Dennis—

A MIDSUMMER NOON IN THE AUSTRALIAN FOREST

NOT a sound disturbs the air,
There is quiet everywhere;
Over plains and over woods
What a mighty stillness broods!

All the birds and insects keep
Where the coolest shadows sleep;
Even the busy ants are found
Resting in their pebbled mound;
Even the locust clingeth now
Silent to the barky bough:
Over hills and over plains
Quiet, vast and slumbrous, reigns.

Only there's a drowsy humming
From yon warm lagoon slow coming:
'Tis the dragon-hornet — see!
All bedaubed resplendently,
Yellow on a tawny ground —
Each rich spot nor square nor round,
Rudely heart-shaped, as it were

The blurred and hasty impress there
Of a vermeil-crusted seal
Dusted o'er with golden meal.
Only there's a droning where
Yon bright beetle shines in air,
Tracks it in its gleaming flight
With a slanting beam of light,
Rising in the sunshine higher,
Till its shards flame out like fire.

Every other thing is still,
Save the ever-wakeful rill,
Whose cool murmur only throws
Cooler comfort round repose;
Or some ripple in the sea
Of leafy boughs, where, lazily,
Tired summer, in her bower
Turning with the noontide hour,
Heaves a slumbrous breath ere she
Once more slumbers peacefully.

O 'tis easeful here to lie
Hidden from noon's scorching eye,
In this grassy cool recess
Musing thus of quietness.

—Charles Harpur—

THE OVERLANDER

THERE'S a trade you all know well —
It's bringing cattle over —
I'll tell you all about the time
When I became a drover.
I made up my mind to try the spec,
To the Clarence I did wander,
And brought a mob of duffers there
To begin as an overlander.

Chorus
Pass the wine cup round, my boys;
Don't let the bottle stand there,
For tonight we'll drink the health
Of every overlander.

When the cattle were all mustered,
And the outfit ready to start,
I saw the lads all mounted,
With their swags left in the cart.
All kinds of men I had
From France, Germany, and Flanders;
Lawyers, doctors, good and bad,
In the mob of overlanders.

From the road I then fed out
When the grass was green and
    young;
When a squatter with curse and
    shout
Told me to move along.
I said, 'You're very hard;
Take care, don't raise my dander,

For I'm a regular knowing card,
The Queensland overlander.'

'Tis true we pay no licence,
And our run is rather large;
'Tis not often they can catch us,
So they cannot make a charge.
They think we live on store beef,
But no, I'm not a gander;
When a good fat stranger joins the
     mob,
'He'll do,' says the overlander.

One day a squatter rode up,
Says he, 'Your on my run;
I've got two boys as witnesses.
Consider your stock in pound.'

I tried to coax, thence bounce him,
But my tin I had to squander,
For he put threepence a head
On the mob of the overlander.

The pretty girls in Brisbane
Were hanging out their duds.
I wished to have a chat with them,
So steered straight for the tubs.
Some dirty urchins saw me,
And soon they raised my dander,
Crying, 'Mother, quick! take in the
    clothes,
Here comes an overlander!'

In town we drain the wine cup,
And go to see the play,

And never think to be hard up
For how to pass the day.
Each has a sweetheart there,
Dressed out in all her grandeur —
Dark eyes and jet black flowing hair.
'She's a plum,' says the overlander.

—Anon—

WHERE THE PELICAN BUILDS

THE horses were ready, the rails
   were down,
But the riders lingered still —
One had a parting word to say,

And one had his pipe to fill.
Then they mounted, one with a
    granted prayer,
And one with a grief unguessed.
'We are going,' they said as they
    rode away,
'Where the pelican builds her nest!'

They had told us of pastures wide
    and green,
To be sought past the sunset's glow;
Of rifts in the ranges by opal lit;
And gold 'neath the river's flow.
And thirst and hunger were
    banished words
When they spoke of the unknown West;

No drought they dreaded, no flood
   they feared,
Where the pelican builds her nest!

The creek at the ford was but fetlock
   deep
When we watched them crossing there;
The rains have replenished it thrice
   since then,
And thrice has the rock lain bare.
But the waters of Hope have flowed
   and fled,
And never from blue hill's breast
Come back — by the sun and the
   sands devoured —
Where the pelican builds her nest.

—Mary Hannay Foott—

WALTZING MATILDA

OH! There once was a swagman
   camped by a billabong,
Under the shade of a coolibah-tree;
And he sang as he looked at his old
   billy boiling,
'Who'll come a-waltzing Matilda
   with me?'

Chorus
Who'll come a-waltzing Matilda, my
   darling,
Who'll come a-waltzing Matilda
   with me?
Waltzing Matilda and leading a
   water-bag —

Who'll come a-waltzing Matilda
   with me?

Down came a jumbuck to drink at
   the water-hole,
Up jumped the swagman and
   grabbed him with glee;
And he sang as he stowed him away
   in his tucker-bag,
'You'll come a-waltzing Matilda
   with me!'

Down came the squatter a-riding his
   thoroughbred;
Down came policemen — one, two,
   and three.

'Whose is the jumbuck you've got in
   the tucker-bag?
You'll come a-waltzing Matilda
   with me'

But the swagman he up and he
   jumped in the water-hole,
Drowning himself by the
   coolibah-tree;
And his ghost may be heard as it
   sings in the billabong,
'Who'll come a-waltzing Matilda with
   me?'

—A.B. ('Banjo') Paterson—

THE TRAVELLER

AS I rode in to Burrumbeet,
I met a man with funny feet;
And, when I paused to ask him why
His feet were strange, he rolled his
    eye
And said the rain would spoil the
    wheat;
So I rode on to Burrumbeet.

As I rode in to Beetaloo,
I met a man whose nose was blue;
And, when I asked him how he got
A nose like that, he answered, 'What
Do bullocks mean when they say Moo?'
So I rode on to Beetaloo.

As I rode in to Ballarat,
I met a man who wore no hat;
And, when I said he might take cold,
He cried, 'The hills are quite as old
As yonder plains, but not so flat.'
So I rode on to Ballarat.

As I rode in to Gundagai,
I met a man and passed him by
Without a nod, without a word.
He turned, and said he'd never
  heard
Or seen a man so wise as I.
But I rode on to Gundagai.

As I rode homeward, full of doubt,
I met a stranger riding out:

A foolish man he seemed to me;
But, 'Nay, I am yourself,' said he,
'Just as you were when you rode out.'
So I rode homeward, free of doubt.

—C.J. Dennis—

THE BANKS OF THE CONDAMINE

OH, hark the dogs are barking, love,
I can no longer stay,
The men are all gone mustering
And it is nearly day.
And I must be off by the morning
    light
Before the sun doth shine,
To meet the Sydney shearers
On the banks of the Condamine.

Oh Willie, dearest Willie,
I'll go along with you,
I'll cut off all my auburn fringe
And be a shearer, too,

I'll cook and count your tally, love,
While ringer-o you shine,
And I'll wash your greasy moleskins
On the banks of the Condamine.

Oh, Nancy, dearest Nancy,
With me you cannot go,
The squatters have given orders,
    love,
No women should do so;
Your delicate constitution
Is not equal unto mine,
To stand the constant tigering
On the banks of the Condamine.

Oh Willie, dearest Willie,
Then stay back home with me,

We'll take up a selection
And a farmer's wife I'll be:
I'll help you husk the corn, love,
And cook your meals so fine
You'll forget the ram-stag mutton
On the banks of the Condamine.

Oh, Nancy, dearest Nancy,
Please do not hold me back,
Down there the boys are waiting,
And I must be on the track;
So here's a good-bye kiss, love,
Back home here I'll incline
When we've shore the last of the
    jumbucks
On the banks of the Condamine.

—Anon—

ANDY'S GONE WITH CATTLE

OUR Andy's gone with cattle now —
Our hearts are out of order —
With drought he's gone to battle now
Across the Queensland border.

He's left us in dejection now;
Our thoughts with him are roving;
It's dull on this selection now,
Since Andy went a-droving.

Who now shall wear the cheerful face
In times when things are slackest?
And who shall whistle round the place
When Fortune frowns her blackest?

Oh, who shall cheek the squatter
    now
When he comes round us snarling?
His tongue is growing hotter now
Since Andy crossed the Darling.

Oh, may the showers in torrents fall,
And all the tanks run over;
And may the grass grow green and
    tall
In pathways of the drover;

And may good angels send the rain
On desert stretches sandy;
And when the summer comes again
God grant 'twill bring us Andy.

—Henry Lawson—

From YE WEARY WAYFARER

HARK! the bells on distant cattle
Waft across the range,
Through the golden-tufted wattle
Music low and strange;
Like the marriage peal of fairies
Comes the tinkling sound,
Or like chimes of sweet St Mary's
On far English ground.

How my courser champs the snaffle,
And with nostrils spread,
Snorts and scarcely seems to ruffle
Fern leaves with his tread;
Cool and pleasant on his haunches
Blows the evening breeze,

Through the overhanging branches
Of the wattle trees;

Onward! to the Southern Ocean
Glides the breath of Spring.
Onward! with a dreamy motion,
I, too, glide and sing —
Forward! forward! still we wander —
Tinted hills that lie
In the red horizon yonder —
Is the goal so nigh?

Whisper, spring-wind, softly singing,
Whisper in my ear;
Respite and nepenthe bringing,
Can the goal be near?
Laden with the dew of vespers,

From the fragrant sky,
In my ear the wind that whispers
Seems to make reply —

'Question not, but live and labour
Till the goal be won,
Helping every feeble neighbour,
Seeking help from none;
Life is mostly froth and bubble,
Two things stand like stone,
Kindness is another's trouble,
Courage in your own.'

—Adam Lindsay Gordon—

THE DYING STOCKMAN

A STRAPPING young stockman lay
  dying,
His saddle supporting his head;
His two mates around him were
  crying,
As he rose on his elbow and said:

Chorus
'Wrap me up with my stockwhip and
  blanket,
And bury me deep down below,
Where the dingoes and crows can't
  molest me,
In then shade where the coolibahs
  grow.

'Oh! had I the flight of the bronze-wing,
Far o'er the plains I would fly,
Straight to the land of my childhood,
And there I would lay down and die.

'Then cut down a couple of saplings,
Place one at my head and my toe,
Carve on them cross, stockwhip, and
    saddle,
To show there's a stockman below.

'Hark! there's a wail of a dingo,
Watchful and weird — I must go,
For it tolls the death-knell of the
    stockman
From the gloom of the scrub down
    below.

'There's tea in the battered old billy;
Place the pannikins out in a row,
And we'll drink to the next merry
    meeting,
In the place where all the good
    fellows go.

'And oft in the shades of the twilight,
When the soft winds are whispering
    low,
And the darkening shadows are
    falling,
Sometimes think of the stockman
    below.'

—Anon—

OLD BOTANY BAY

I'M OLD
Botany Bay;
Stiff in the joints,
Little to say.

I am he
Who paved the way,
That you might walk
At your ease today;
I was the conscript
Sent to hell
To make in the desert
The living well;

I bore the heat,

I blazed the track —
Furrowed and bloody
Upon my back.

I split the rock;
I felled the tree:
The nation was —
Because of me!

Old Botany Bay
Taking the sun
From day to day...
Shame on the mouth
That would deny
The knotted hands
That set us high!

—Mary Gilmore—

THE LAST OF HIS TRIBE

HE crouches and buries his head on
    his knees,
And hides in the dark of his hair;
For he cannot look up to the
    storm-smitten trees,
Or think of the loneliness there —
Of the loss and the loneliness there.

The wallaroos grope through the
    tufts of the grass,
And turn to their coverts for fear;
But he sits in the ashes and lets them
    pass
Where the boomerangs sleep with the
    spear —

With the nullah, the sling, and the
  spear.

Uloola, behold him! The thunder
  that breaks
On the tops of the rocks with the
  rain,
And the wind which drives up with
  the salt of the lakes,
Have made him a hunter again —
A hunter and fisher again.

For his eyes have been full with a
smouldering thought;
But he dreams of the hunts of yore,
And of foes that he sought, and of
  fights that he fought

With those who will battle no more —
Who will go to the battle no more.

It is well that the water which
   tumbles and fills
Goes moaning and moaning along;
For an echo rolls out from the sides
   of the hills,
And he starts at a wonderful song —
At a sound of a wonderful song.

And he sees through the rents of the
   scattering fogs
The corroboree warlike and grim,
And the lubra who sat by the fire on
   the logs,
To watch, like a mourner, for him —

Like a mother and mourner for him.

Will he go in his sleep from these
    desolate lands,
Like a chief, to the rest of his race,
With the honey-voiced woman who
    beckons and stands,
And gleams like a dream in his face —
Like a marvellous dream in his face?

—Henry Kendall—

SPRING ON THE PLAINS

SPRING has come to the plains,
And, following close behind,
Green of the welcome rains
And spice of the first warm wind.
Beating of wings on high,
For, overhead in the blue,
Southward the brolgas fly,
The cranes and pelicans, too,
Ibis and proud black swan —
And quivering cries float clear,
After the birds are gone
Still lingering in the ear.

Everywhere we pass
The horses tread soft and deep;

Clover and young green grass —
Hark to the grazing sheep
Cropping steady and slow —
A peaceful, satisfied sound:
Thick on the paths we go,
Gold flowers are starring the ground.
Spring, and the world's astir,
And everything gives praise,
Singing the strength of her
These lovely lengthening days.

—Dorothea Mackellar—

ACKNOWLEDGEMENTS

THE publishers express their gratitude
to the following for permission to
reproduce material in copyright:

Collins/Angus & Robertson Publishers
Australia for 'Old Botany Bay' by Mary
Gilmore from *The Singing Tree*; 'Nine
Miles from Gundagai' by Jack Moses from
Nine Miles from Gundagai; 'The Man from
Snowy River' and Waltzing Matilda' by
A.B. Paterson from *The Collected Verse of
A.B. Paterson*.

Curtis Brown (Australia) and the estate of
the late Dorothea Mackellar for 'My
Country' and 'Spring on the Plains'.